MILITARY SCIENCE

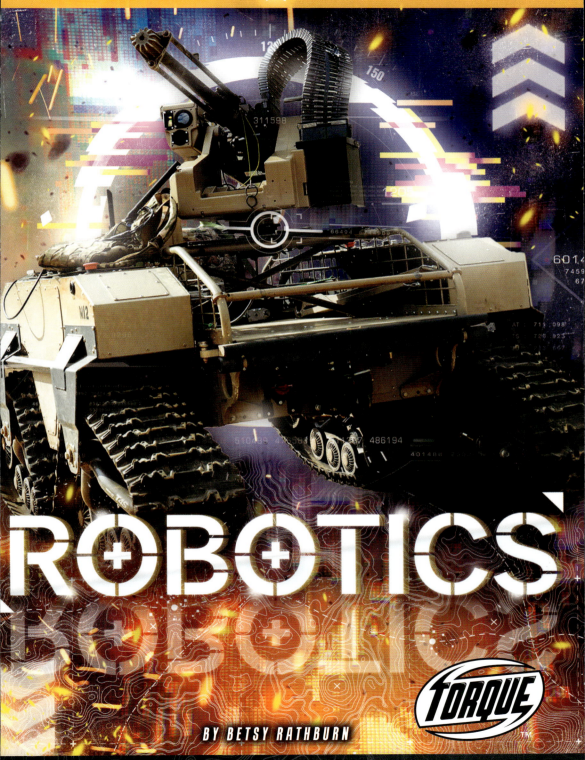

ROBOTICS

BY BETSY RATHBURN

BELLWETHER MEDIA • MINNEAPOLIS, MN

Torque brims with excitement perfect for thrill-seekers of all kinds. Discover daring survival skills, explore uncharted worlds, and marvel at mighty engines and extreme sports. In *Torque* books, anything can happen. Are you ready?

This edition first published in 2022 by Bellwether Media, Inc.

No part of this publication may be reproduced in whole or in part without written permission of the publisher. For information regarding permission, write to Bellwether Media, Inc., Attention: Permissions Department, 6012 Blue Circle Drive, Minnetonka, MN 55343.

Library of Congress Cataloging-in-Publication Data

Names: Rathburn, Betsy, author.
Title: Robotics / by Betsy Rathburn.
Description: Minneapolis, MN : Bellwether Media, 2022. | Series: Torque: Military science | Includes bibliographical references and index. | Audience: Ages 7-12 | Audience: Grades 4-6 | Summary: "Amazing photography accompanies engaging information about military robotics. The combination of high-interest subject matter and light text is intended for students in grades 3 through 7"–Provided by publisher.
Identifiers: LCCN 2021051725 (print) | LCCN 2021051726 (ebook) | ISBN 9781644876305 (library binding) | ISBN 9781648346415 (ebook)
Subjects: LCSH: Military robots–Juvenile literature.
Classification: LCC UG450 .R38 2022 (print) | LCC UG450 (ebook) | DDC 629.8/92–dc23/eng/20211020
LC record available at https://lccn.loc.gov/2021051725
LC ebook record available at https://lccn.loc.gov/2021051726

Text copyright © 2022 by Bellwether Media, Inc. TORQUE and associated logos are trademarks and/or registered trademarks of Bellwether Media, Inc.

Editor: Elizabeth Neuenfeldt   Designer: Jeffrey Kollock

Printed in the United States of America, North Mankato, MN.

TABLE OF CONTENTS

BOMB SQUAD	4
WHAT IS ROBOTICS?	6
THE SCIENCE BEHIND ROBOTICS	12
THE FUTURE OF ROBOTICS	18
GLOSSARY	22
TO LEARN MORE	23
INDEX	24

BOMB SQUAD

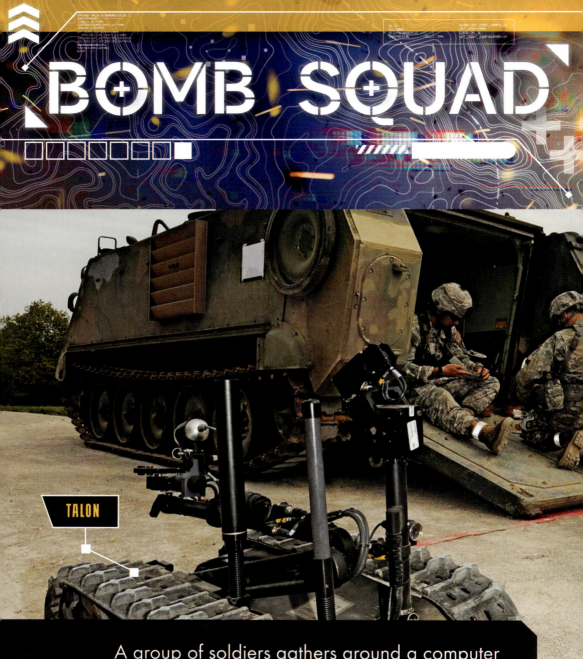

TALON

A group of soldiers gathers around a computer screen. One soldier holds a remote control. He uses it to direct a TALON over rough ground.

4

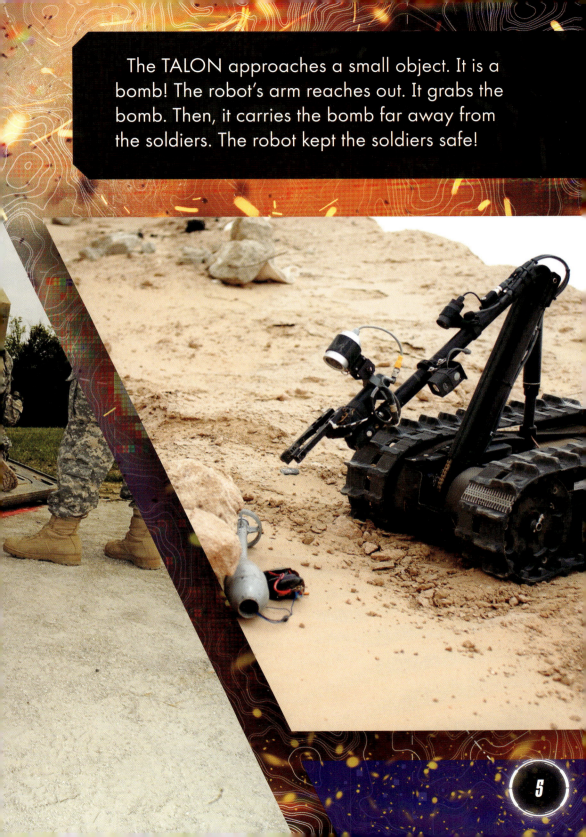

The TALON approaches a small object. It is a bomb! The robot's arm reaches out. It grabs the bomb. Then, it carries the bomb far away from the soldiers. The robot kept the soldiers safe!

WHAT IS ROBOTICS?

Robotics is the use of robots to do military work. The military uses robots to make work easier and safer. This gives troops time to do other important work.

The earliest military robots were small **tanks**. They were built in the 1940s. Since then, scientists have worked hard to make new military robots!

TIMELINE

1942 — GOLIATH TRACKED MINE

1995 — MQ-1 PREDATOR

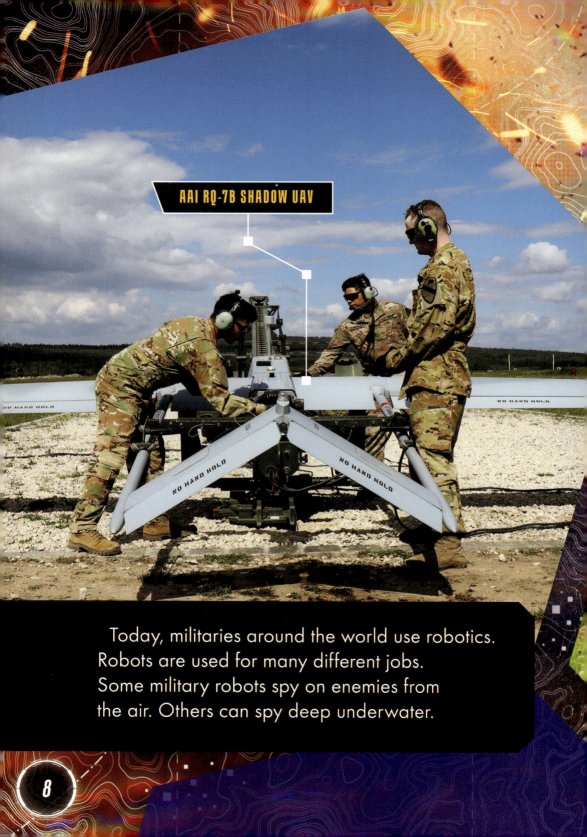

AAI RQ-7B SHADOW UAV

Today, militaries around the world use robotics. Robots are used for many different jobs. Some military robots spy on enemies from the air. Others can spy deep underwater.

Military robots also guard protected areas, build things, and carry heavy loads. Some robots are used for search and rescue jobs.

SUPPLY ROBOT

The military has tested many robots. The LS3 was made to carry heavy supplies for troops. But it was too loud to be used!

LS3

The military uses many types of robots. **Unmanned aerial vehicles** (UAVs) fly over enemy land. They take pictures and record videos. Some even carry weapons.

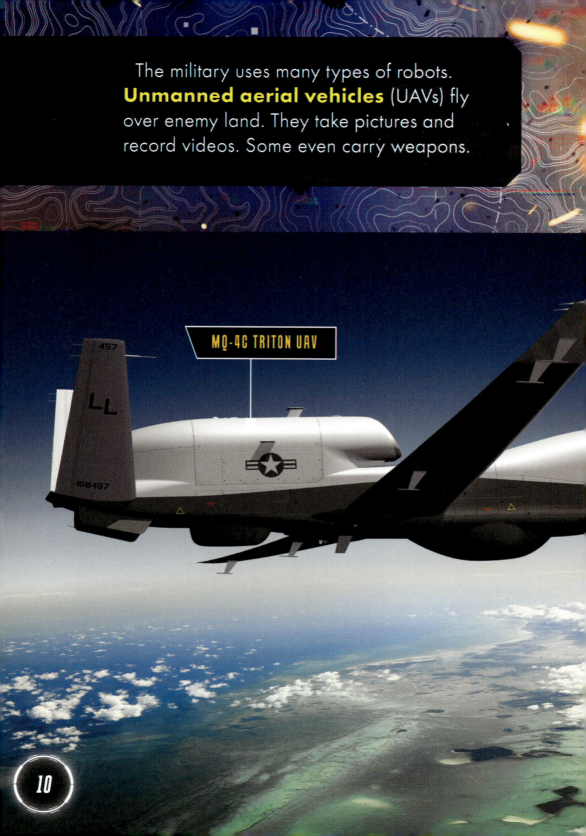

MQ-4C TRITON UAV

ROBOTICS PROFILE

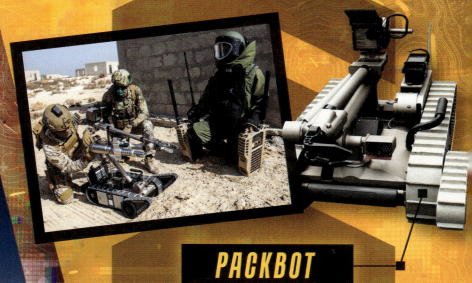

PACKBOT

DEVELOPED: STARTED IN 1998

FEATURES: UGV WITH TRACKS, ARMS, AND CAMERAS USED TO GATHER INFORMATION AND GET RID OF BOMBS

Unmanned ground vehicles (UGVs) travel over land. They squeeze into small spaces and check out dangerous areas. **Unmanned underwater vehicles** (UUVs) work underwater. They gather information and hunt for **mines**!

THE SCIENCE BEHIND ROBOTICS

Troops control robots from a distance. They use remote controls or computers. These tools have **transmitters**. They send directions as **radio waves**.

12

HOW ROBOTS GET SIGNALS

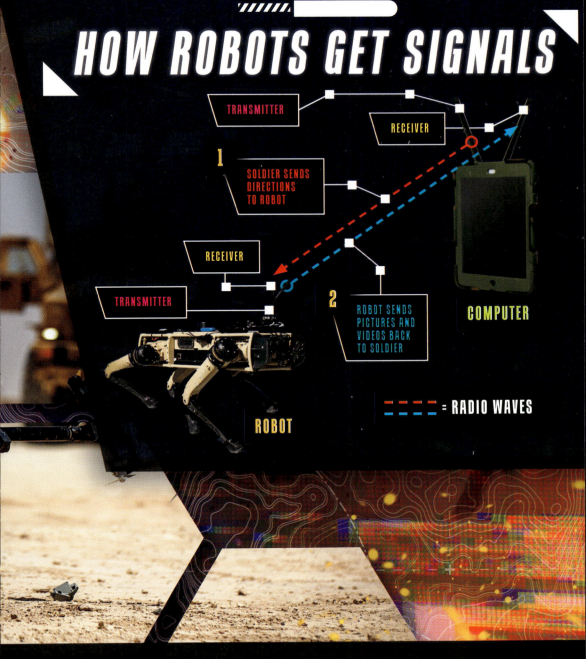

The robot's **receiver** picks up the directions. The robot is **programmed** to follow them. It sends pictures and videos back to the controller.

Each type of robot has different parts. UGVs often have **tracks**. Tracks help UGVs travel over rough ground. Strong arms help them lift heavy items. Blades push and lift dirt.

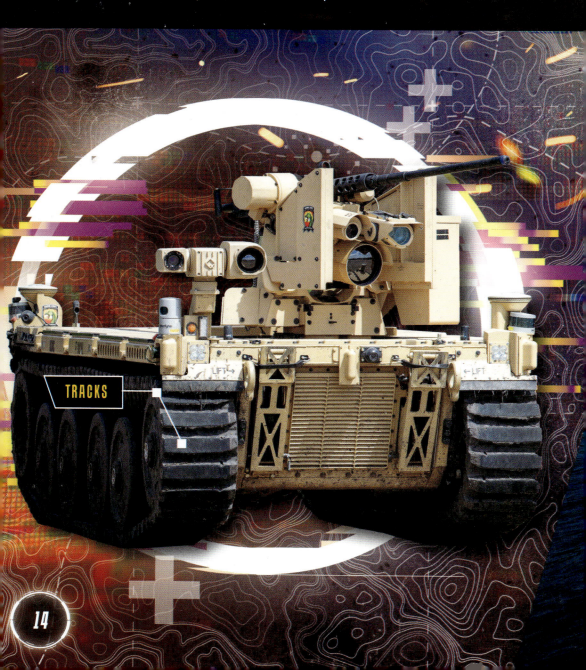

TRACKS

UUVs are built with strong materials to dive deep. **Propellers** help them move underwater.

UUV

PROPELLER

PROPELLER

UAVs have propellers, too. The curved blades help UAVs fly. Some UAVs have wings to stay balanced in the air. Powerful batteries allow UAVs to travel for many hours without stopping.

16

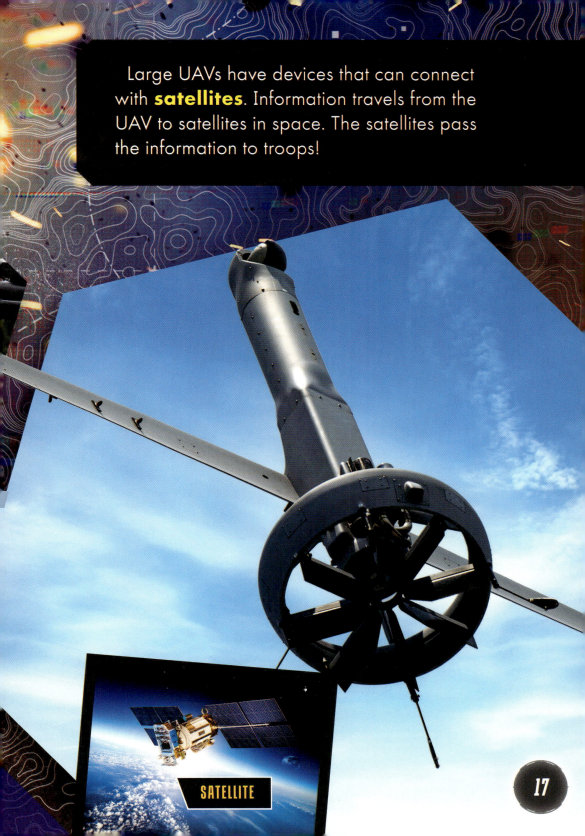

Large UAVs have devices that can connect with **satellites**. Information travels from the UAV to satellites in space. The satellites pass the information to troops!

SATELLITE

THE FUTURE OF ROBOTICS

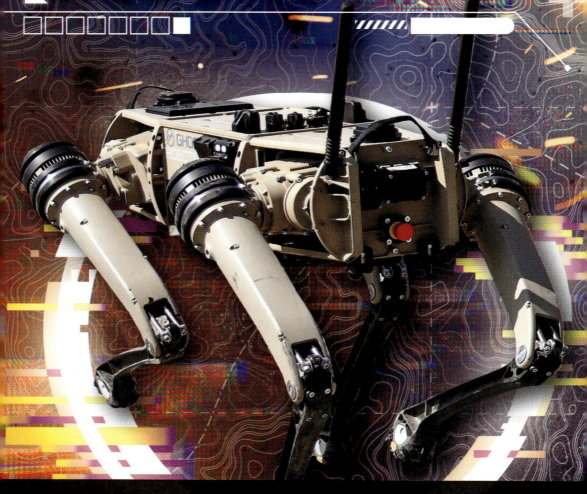

Scientists are working on new technology to make robots more powerful. Robots will also be able to do new jobs.

FUTURE ROBOTICS PROFILE

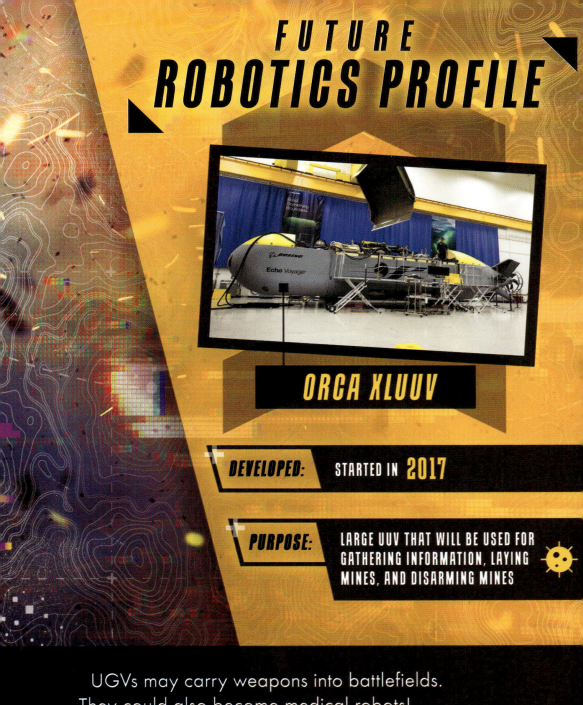

ORCA XLUUV

DEVELOPED: STARTED IN 2017

PURPOSE: LARGE UUV THAT WILL BE USED FOR GATHERING INFORMATION, LAYING MINES, AND DISARMING MINES

UGVs may carry weapons into battlefields. They could also become medical robots! Cameras would let doctors check injured soldiers from a distance. Doctors could also use the robots to wrap wounds or give medicine!

Future robots may even use **AI**. They would not be controlled by a person. Instead, they would be programmed to make decisions on their own. They would do their jobs without human help.

NON-MILITARY USES

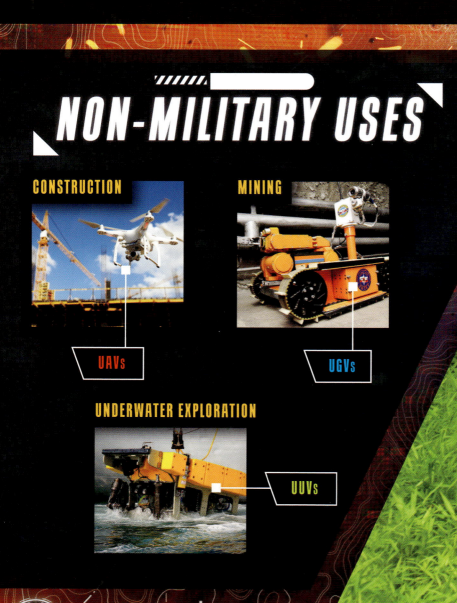

CONSTRUCTION

UAVs

MINING

UGVs

UNDERWATER EXPLORATION

UUVs

WEARABLE ROBOTS

Wearable robotics is also possible! Scientists are creating powerful suits for troops to wear. The suits will make troops stronger!

Militaries will keep making better robots. The future of robotics has many possibilities!

GLOSSARY

AI—artificial intelligence; AI is the ability of machines to copy human actions.

mines—weapons that are buried underground or underwater and explode when something touches them

programmed—provided with instructions to do a certain thing

propellers—spinning parts that make some machines move

radio waves—energy waves that are used for long-distance communication

receiver—a device that picks up radio waves

satellites—human-made objects that circle Earth; satellites are used to communicate and study Earth.

tanks—armored vehicles that carry guns

tracks—metal bands around the wheels of some vehicles

transmitters—devices that send out radio waves

unmanned aerial vehicles—vehicles in the air that are controlled by people who are not on board; they are often called UAVs.

unmanned ground vehicles—vehicles on the ground that are controlled by people who are not on board; they are often called UGVs.

unmanned underwater vehicles—vehicles in the water that are controlled by people who are not on board; they are often called UUVs.

TO LEARN MORE

AT THE LIBRARY

Bassier, Emma. *Military Robots*. Minneapolis, Minn.: Pop!, 2020.

Chandler, Matt. *Drones*. Minneapolis, Minn.: Bellwether Media, 2022.

Gitlin, Marty. *Submarines*. Hallandale, Fla.: Mitchell Lane, 2021.

ON THE WEB

Factsurfer.com gives you a safe, fun way to find more information.

1. Go to www.factsurfer.com

2. Enter "robotics" into the search box and click 🔍.

3. Select your book cover to see a list of related content.

INDEX

AI, 20
arms, 5, 14
batteries, 16
blades, 14, 16
bomb, 5
cameras, 19
computer, 4, 12
future, 18, 19, 20, 21
how robots get signals, 13
jobs, 8, 9, 10, 11, 18, 19, 20
LS3, 9
mines, 11
non-military uses, 20
Orca XLUUV, 19
PackBot, 11
pictures, 10, 13
propellers, 15, 16
radio waves, 12
receiver, 13
remote control, 4, 12, 13
satellites, 17
soldiers, 4, 5, 19

TALON, 4, 5
tanks, 6
timeline, 6–7
tracks, 14
transmitters, 12
troops, 6, 9, 12, 17, 21
unmanned aerial vehicles, 10, 16, 17
unmanned ground vehicles, 11, 14, 19
unmanned underwater vehicles, 11, 15, 19
videos, 10, 13
weapons, 10, 19
wearable robotics, 21
wings, 16

The images in this book are reproduced through the courtesy of: Sgt. Julien Rodarte/ DVIDS, front cover; PJF Military Collection/ Alamy, p. 3; United States Military/ flickr, pp. 4-5; Sgt. Giancarlo Caseum/ DVIDS, p. 5; baku13/ Wikimedia Commons, p. 6 (1942); Lt. Col. Leslie Pratt/ Wikimedia Commons, p. 6 (1995); leshiy985, pp. 7 (2000), 23; Armyinform.com.ua/ Wikimedia Commons, p. 7 (2020); Luke Allen/ DVIDS, pp. 6-7, 14; Gregory Stevens/ DVIDS, pp. 8-9 (left); Sarah Anderson/ DVIDS, pp. 8-9 (right); CNP Collection/ Alamy, pp. 10-11; U.S. Navy/ Wikimedia Commons, p. 11; viper-zero, p. 11 (isolated); Spc. Derek Mustard/ DVIDS, pp. 12-13; Boeing Images/ Boeing Media Room, pp. 14-15, 19; Gabriel Silva/ DVIDS, pp. 16-17 (left); Anderson W Branch/ DVIDS, pp. 16-17 (right); Andrey Armyagov, p. 17 (inset); Cynthia Griggs/ DIVDS, p. 18; Dmitry Kalinovsky, p. 20 (UAV); ITAR-TASS News Agency/ Alamy, p. 20 (UGV); Victor Ivin, p. 20 (UUV); David McNally/ DVIDS, pp. 20-21.

24